THE LITTLE LIBRARY OF EARTH MEDICINE

SALMON

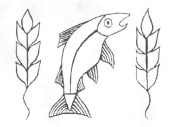

Kenneth Meadows

Illustrations by Jo Donegan

DK PUBLISHING, INC.

A DK PUBLISHING BOOK

The Little Library of Earth Medicine was
produced, edited, and designed by
GLS Editorial and Design
Garden Studios, 11-15 Betterton Street
London WC2H 9BP

Editorial director: Jane Laing
Design director: Ruth Shane
Project designer: Luke Herriott
Editors: Claire Calman, Terry Burrows, Victoria Sorzano
US Editors: Jennifer Dorr, William Lach, Barbara Minton

Additional illustrations: Roy Flooks 16, 17, 31; John Lawrence 38
Special photography: Mark Hamilton
Picture credits: American Natural History Museum 8-9, 12, 14-15;
San Diego Museum of Man (photograph by John Oldenkamp) 32

First American Edition, 1998
2 4 6 8 10 9 7 5 3 1

Published in the United States by DK Publishing, Inc.
95 Madison Avenue, New York, NY 10016
Visit us on the World Wide Web at http://www.dk.com.

Copyright © 1998 Dorling Kindersley Limited, London
Text © 1998 Kenneth Meadows

Library of Congress Cataloging-in-Publication Data
Meadows, Kenneth.
 The little library of earth medicine / by Kenneth Meadows. – 1st American ed.
  p. cm.
 Contents: |1| Falcon, 21st March-19th April – |2| Beaver, 20th April-20 May – |3|
Deer, 21st May-20th June – |4| Woodpecker, 21st June-21st July – |5| Salmon, 22nd July-
21st August – |6| Brown Bear, 22nd August-21st September – |7| Crow, 22nd
September-22nd October – |8| Snake, 23rd October-22nd November – |9| Owl, 23rd
November-21st December – |10| Goose, 22nd December-19 January – |11| Otter, 20th
January-18th February – |12| Wolf, 19th February-20th March.
 Includes indexes.
 ISBN 0-7894-2876-8
 1. Medicine wheels–Miscellanea. 2. Horoscopes. 3. Indians of North
America–Religion–Miscellanea. 4. Typology (Psychology)–Miscellanea. I. Title.
BF1623.M43M42 1998
133.5'9397–dc21   97-42267
                                                          CIP

Reproduced by Kestrel Digital Colour Ltd. Chelmsford, Essex
Printed and bound in Hong Kong by Imago

CONTENTS

SALMON MEDICINE 25

INTRODUCING
EARTH MEDICINE

To Native Americans, medicine is not an external substance but an inner power that is found in both Nature and ourselves.

E arth Medicine is a unique method of personality profiling that draws on Native American understanding of the Universe, and on the principles embodied in sacred Medicine Wheels.

Native Americans believed that spirit, although invisible, permeated Nature, so that everything in Nature was sacred. Animals were perceived as acting as

messengers of spirit. They also appeared in waking dreams to impart power known as "medicine." The recipients of such dreams honored the animal species that appeared to them by rendering their images on ceremonial, ornamental, and everyday artifacts.

NATURE WITHIN SELF

Native American shamans – tribal wisemen – recognized similarities between the natural forces prevalent during the seasons and the characteristics of those born

Shaman's rattle
Shamans used rattles to connect with their inner spirit. This is a Tlingit shaman's wooden rattle.

"Spirit has provided you with an opportunity to study in Nature's university." *Stoney teaching*

during corresponding times of the year. They also noted how personality is affected by the four phases of the Moon – at birth and throughout life – and by the continual alternation of energy flow, from active to passive. This view is encapsulated in Earth Medicine, which helps you to recognize how the dynamics of Nature function within you and how the potential strengths you were born with can be developed.

Animal ornament
To the Anasazi, who carved this ornament from jet, the frog symbolized adaptability.

MEDICINE WHEELS

Native American cultural traditions embrace a variety of circular symbolic images and objects. These sacred hoops have become known as Medicine

Wheels, due to their similarity to the spoked wheels of the wagons that carried settlers into the heartlands of once-Native American territory. Each Medicine Wheel showed how different objects or qualities related to one another within the context of a greater whole, and how different forces and energies moved within it.

One Medicine Wheel might be regarded as the master wheel because it indicated balance within Nature and the most effective way of achieving harmony with the Universe and ourselves. It is upon this master Medicine Wheel (see pp.10–11) that Earth Medicine is structured.

Feast dish
Stylized bear carvings adorn this Tlingit feast dish. To the Native American, the bear symbolizes strength and self-sufficiency.

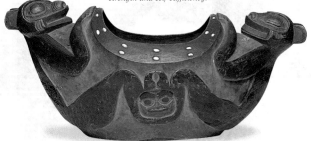

THE MEDICINE WHEEL

The outer Wheel is divided into twelve birth times, each of which has its own animal totem, and stone, tree, and color affinities.

At the hub of the Wheel, surrounded by representations of Elements, Directions, and energy flow, is the Wakan-Tanka – symbol of invisible energies coming into physical reality.

Season of birth
Each of the twelve segments relates to a specific time of year (see pp.12–13).

Wakan-Tanka
The powerful symbol used by some Native Americans to denote energy coming into form (see p.24).

NORTH: WINTER

WEST: AUTUMN

WOLF

OTTER

GOOSE

OWL

SNAKE

CROW

Stone affinity
Each birth time has a particular stone associated with it (see pp.14–15).

Tree affinity
Each birth time is connected to a type of tree (see pp.14–15).

Birth totem
An animal totem represents each birth time (see pp.16–17).

Directional totem
One of four cardinal Directions exerts an influence on each birth time (see pp.18–19).

Principal Element
Each birth time is fundamentally influenced by one of the four Elements (see pp.20–21).

Energy flow
Energy alternates between active and receptive with each birth time (see p.24).

Elemental Aspect
Each birth time has its own Elemental Aspect (see pp.20–21).

EAST: SPRING

FALCON

BEAVER

DEER

DEER

WOODPECKER

SALMON

BROWN BEAR

South: SUMMER

11

THE TWELVE
BIRTH TIMES

THE STRUCTURE OF THE MEDICINE WHEEL IS BASED
UPON THE SEASONS TO REFLECT THE POWERFUL
INFLUENCE OF NATURE ON HUMAN PERSONALITY.

T he Medicine Wheel classifies human nature into twelve personality types, each corresponding to the characteristics of Nature at a particular time of the year. It is designed to act as a kind of map to help you discover your strengths and weaknesses, your inner drives and instinctive behaviors, and your true potential.

The four seasons form the basis of the Wheel's structure, with the Summer and Winter solstices and the Spring and Autumn equinoxes marking each season's passing. In Earth Medicine,

Seasonal rites

Performers at the Iroquois mid-Winter ceremony wore masks made of braided maize husks. They danced to attune themselves to energies that would ensure a good harvest.

each season is a metaphor for a stage of human growth and development. Spring is likened to infancy and the newness of life; and Summer to the exuberance of youth and of rapid development. Autumn represents the fulfillment that mature adulthood brings, while Winter symbolizes the accumulated wisdom that can be drawn upon in later life.

Each seasonal quarter of the Wheel is further divided into three periods, making twelve time segments altogether. The time of your birth determines the direction from which

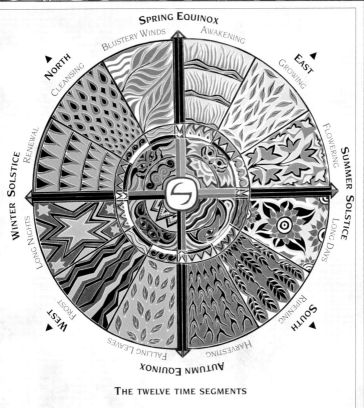

THE TWELVE TIME SEGMENTS

you perceive life, and the qualities imbued in Nature in that season are reflected in your core character.

Each of the twelve time segments, or birth times, is named after a feature in the natural yearly cycle. For example, the period after the Spring equinox is called Awakening time because it is the time of new growth, while the segment after the Autumn equinox is named after the falling leaves that characterize that time.

THE SIGNIFICANCE OF
TOTEMS

NATIVE AMERICANS BELIEVED THAT TOTEMS — ANIMAL
SYMBOLS — REPRESENTED ESSENTIAL TRUTHS AND ACTED
AS CONNECTIONS TO NATURAL POWERS.

A totem is an animal or natural object adopted as an emblem to typify certain distinctive qualities. Native Americans regarded animals, whose behavior is predictable, as particularly useful guides to categorizing human patterns of behavior.

A totem mirrors aspects of your nature and unlocks the intuitive knowledge that lies beyond the reasoning capacity of the intellect. It may take the form of a carving or molding, a pictorial image, or a token of fur, feather, bone, tooth, or claw. Its presence serves as an immediate link with the energies it represents. A totem is therefore more effective than a glyph or symbol as an aid to comprehending nonphysical powers and formative forces.

PRIMARY TOTEMS

In Earth Medicine you have three primary totems: a birth totem, a Directional totem, and an Elemental totem. Your *birth totem* is the embodiment of core characteristics that correspond with the dominant aspects of Nature during your birth time.

Symbol of strength

The handle of this Tlingit knife is carved with a raven and a bear head, symbols of insight and inner strength.

All twelve birth totems, each relating to a birth time, are described on pp.16–17.

Your Directional totem aligns you with your inner senses, which direct the main thrust of your endeavors. Each of the four seasons on the Wheel is compatible with one of the four Directions, and each of the Directions is represented by a totem. For example, Spring is associated with the East, where the sun rises, and signifies seeing things in new ways; its totem is the Eagle. The four

Prize totem

A chief or warrior of the Fox tribe affirmed his rank with this bear claw necklace.

Directional totems are explained on pp.18–19.

Your Elemental totem relates to your instinctive behaviors. The qualities of the four Elements – Fire, Water, Earth, and Air – and their totems are introduced on pp.20–21.

THREE AFFINITIES

Each birth time also has an affinity with a tree, a stone, and a color (see pp.36–41). These three affinities have qualities that can strengthen you during challenging times.

"If a man is to succeed, he must be governed not by his inclination, but by an understanding of the ways of animals..." Teton Sioux teaching

THE TWELVE
BIRTH TOTEMS

THE TWELVE BIRTH TIMES ARE REPRESENTED BY TOTEMS,
EACH ONE AN ANIMAL THAT BEST EXPRESSES THE
QUALITIES INHERENT IN THAT BIRTH TIME.

E arth Medicine associates an animal totem with each birth time (the two sets of dates below reflect the difference in season between the Northern and Southern Hemispheres). These animals help to connect you to the powers and abilities that they represent. For an in-depth study of the Salmon birth totem, see pp.28–29.

FALCON
March 21–April 19 (N. Hem)
Sept 22–Oct 22 (S. Hem)
Falcons are full of initiative, but often rush in to make decisions they may later regret. Lively and extroverted, they have enthusiasm for new experiences but can sometimes lack persistence.

DEER
May 21–June 20 (N. Hem)
Nov 23–Dec 21 (S. Hem)
Deer are willing to sacrifice the old for the new. They loathe routine, thriving on variety and challenges. They have a wild side, often leaping from one situation or relationship into another without reflection.

BEAVER
April 20–May 20 (N. Hem)
Oct 23–Nov 22 (S. Hem)
Practical and steady, Beavers have a capacity for perseverance. Good homemakers, they are warm and affectionate but need harmony and peace to avoid becoming irritable. They have a keen aesthetic sense.

WOODPECKER
June 21–July 21 (N. Hem)
Dec 22–Jan 19 (S. Hem)
Emotional and sensitive, Woodpeckers are warm to those closest to them, and willing to sacrifice their needs for those of their loved ones. They have lively imaginations but can be worriers.

SALMON

July 22 – August 21 (N. Hem)
Jan 20 – Feb 18 (S. Hem)

Enthusiastic and self-confident, Salmon people enjoy running things. They are uncompromising and forceful, and can occasionally seem a little arrogant or self-important. They are easily hurt by neglect.

BROWN BEAR

August 22 – Sept 21 (N. Hem)
Feb 19 – March 20 (S. Hem)

Brown Bears are hardworking, practical, and self-reliant. They do not like change, preferring to stick to what is familiar. They have a flair for fixing things, are good-natured, and make good friends.

CROW

Sept 22 – Oct 22 (N. Hem)
March 21 – April 19 (S. Hem)

Crows dislike solitude and feel most comfortable in company. Although usually pleasant and good-natured, they can be strongly influenced by negative atmospheres, becoming gloomy and prickly.

SNAKE

Oct 23 – Nov 22 (N. Hem)
April 20 – May 20 (S. Hem)

Snakes are secretive and mysterious, hiding their feelings beneath a cool exterior. Adaptable, determined, and imaginative, they are capable of bouncing back from tough situations encountered in life.

OWL

Nov 23 – Dec 21 (N. Hem)
May 21 – June 20 (S. Hem)

Owls need freedom of expression. They are lively, self-reliant, and have an eye for detail. Inquisitive and adaptable, they have a tendency to overextend themselves. Owls are often physically courageous.

GOOSE

Dec 22 – Jan 19 (N. Hem)
June 21 – July 21 (S. Hem)

Goose people are far-sighted idealists who are willing to explore the unknown. They approach life with enthusiasm, determined to fulfill their dreams. They are perfectionists, and can appear unduly serious.

OTTER

Jan 20 – Feb 18 (N. Hem)
July 22 – August 21 (S. Hem)

Otters are friendly, lively, and perceptive. They feel inhibited by too many rules and regulations, which often makes them appear eccentric. They like cleanliness and order, and have original minds.

WOLF

Feb 19 – March 20 (N. Hem)
August 22 – Sept 21 (S. Hem)

Wolves are sensitive, artistic, and intuitive – people to whom others turn for help. They value freedom and their own space, and are easily affected by others. They are philosophical, trusting, and genuine.

THE INFLUENCE OF THE
DIRECTIONS

ALSO KNOWN BY NATIVE AMERICANS AS THE FOUR
WINDS, THE INFLUENCE OF THE FOUR DIRECTIONS IS
EXPERIENCED THROUGH YOUR INNER SENSES.

Regarded as the "keepers" or "caretakers" of the Universe, the four Directions or alignments were also referred to by Native Americans as the four Winds because their presence was felt rather than seen.

DIRECTIONAL TOTEMS

In Earth Medicine, each Direction or Wind is associated with a season and a time of day. Thus the Summer birth times – Long Days time, Ripening time, and Harvesting time – all fall within the South Direction, and afternoon. The Direction to which your birth time belongs influences the nature of your inner senses.

The East Direction is associated with illumination. Its totem is the Eagle – a bird that soars closest to the Sun and can see clearly from height. The South is the Direction of Summer and the afternoon. It signifies growth and fruition, fluidity, and emotions. Its totem, the Mouse, symbolizes productivity, feelings, and an ability to perceive detail.

"Remember...the circle of the sky, the stars, the supernatural Winds breathing night and day...the four Directions." Pawnee teaching

SPRING EQUINOX

NORTH

EAST

WINTER SOLSTICE

SUMMER SOLSTICE

WEST

SOUTH

AUTUMN EQUINOX

BUFFALO

EAGLE

GRIZZLY BEAR

MOUSE

The four Directions

*Each Direction is associated with a
season and a time of day, and also
with a principal function: the East
with determining, the South with
giving, the West with holding, and
the North with receiving.*

The West is the Direction of Autumn
and the evening. It signifies
transformation – from day to night,
from Summer to Winter – and the
qualities of introspection and
conservation. Its totem is the Grizzly
Bear, which represents strength

drawn from within. The North is the
Direction of Winter and the night,
and is associated with the mind and
its sustenance – knowledge. Its
totem is the Buffalo, an animal that
was honored by Native Americans as
the great material "provider."

THE INFLUENCE OF THE
ELEMENTS

THE FOUR ELEMENTS – AIR, FIRE, WATER, AND EARTH –
PERVADE EVERYTHING AND INDICATE THE NATURE OF
MOVEMENT AND THE ESSENCE OF WHO YOU ARE.

E lements are intangible qualities that describe the essential state or character of all things. In Earth Medicine, the four Elements are allied with four fundamental modes of activity and are associated with different aspects of the self. Air expresses free movement in all directions; it is related to the mind and to thinking. Fire indicates expansive motion; it is linked with the spirit and with intuition. Water signifies fluidity; it

Elemental profile
The configuration of Salmon is Fire of Water. Water is the Principal Element and Fire the Elemental Aspect.

EARTH

FIRE

WATER

WATER

FIRE

AIR

has associations with the soul and the emotions. Earth symbolizes stability; it is related to the physical body and the sensations.

ELEMENTAL DISTRIBUTION

On the Medicine Wheel one Element is associated with each of the four Directions – Fire in the East, Earth in the West, Air in the North, and Water in the South. These are known as the Principal Elements.

The four Elements also have an individual association with each of the twelve birth times – known as the Elemental Aspects. They follow a cyclical sequence around the Wheel based on the action of the Sun (Fire) on the Earth, producing atmosphere (Air) and condensation (Water).

The three birth times that share an Elemental Aspect belong to the same Elemental family or "clan," with a totem that gives insight into its key qualities. Salmon people belong to the Hawk clan (see pp.34–35).

ELEMENTAL EMPHASIS

For each birth time, the qualities of the Elemental Aspect usually predominate over those of the Principal Element, although both are present to give a specific configuration, such as Fire of Earth (for Salmon's, see pp.34–35). For Falcon, Woodpecker, and Otter, the Principal Element and the Elemental Aspect are identical (for example, Air of Air), so people of these totems tend to express that Element intensely.

AIR

WATER

EARTH

FIRE

AIR

EARTH

THE INFLUENCE OF THE
MOON

THE WAXING AND WANING OF THE MOON DURING ITS
FOUR PHASES HAS A CRUCIAL INFLUENCE ON THE
FORMATION OF PERSONALITY AND HUMAN ENDEAVOR.

Native Americans regarded the Sun and Moon as indicators respectively of the active and receptive energies inherent in Nature (see p.24), as well as the measurers of time. They associated solar influences with conscious activity and the exercise of reason and the will, and lunar influences with subconscious activity and the emotional and intuitive aspects of human nature.

The Waxing Moon

This phase lasts for approximately eleven days. It is a time of growth and therefore ideal for developing new ideas and concentrating your efforts into new projects.

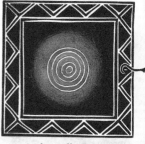

The Full Moon

Lasting about three days, this is when lunar power is at its height. It is therefore a good time for completing what was developed during the Waxing Moon.

THE FOUR PHASES

There are four phases in the twenty-nine-day lunar cycle, each one an expression of energy reflecting a particular mode of activity. They can be likened to the phases of growth of a flowering plant through the seasons: the emergence of buds (Waxing Moon), the bursting of flowers (Full Moon), the falling away of flowers (Waning Moon), and the germination of seeds (Dark Moon). The influence of each phase can be felt in two ways: in the formation of personality and in day-to-day life.

The energy expressed by the phase of the Moon at the time of your birth has a strong influence on personality. For instance, someone born during the Dark Moon is likely to be inward-looking, while a person born during the Full Moon may be more expressive. Someone born during a Waxing Moon is likely to have an outgoing nature, while a person born during a Waning Moon may be reserved. Consult a set of Moon tables to discover the phase the Moon was in on your birthday.

In your day-to-day life, the benefits of coming into harmony with the Moon's energies are considerable. Experience the energy of the four phases by consciously working with them. A Native American approach is described below.

The Waning Moon
A time for making changes, this phase lasts for an average of eleven days. Use it to improve and modify, and to dispose of what is no longer needed or wanted.

The Dark Moon
The Moon disappears from the sky for around four days. This is a time for contemplation of what has been achieved, and for germinating the seeds for the new.

THE INFLUENCE OF ENERGY FLOW

THE MEDICINE WHEEL REFLECTS THE PERFECT BALANCE OF THE COMPLEMENTARY ACTIVE AND RECEPTIVE ENERGIES THAT COEXIST IN NATURE.

Energy flows through Nature in two complementary ways, which can be expressed in terms of active and receptive, or male and female. The active energy principle is linked with the Elements of Fire and Air, and the receptive principle with Water and Earth.

Each of the twelve birth times has an active or receptive energy related to its Elemental Aspect. Traveling around the Wheel, the two energies alternate with each birth time, resulting in an equal balance of active and receptive energies, as in Nature.

Active energy is associated with the Sun and conscious activity. Those whose birth times take this principle prefer to pursue experience. They are conceptual,

energetic, outgoing, practical, and analytical. Receptive energy is associated with the Moon and subconscious activity. Those whose birth times take this principle prefer to attract experience. They are intuitive, reflective, conserving, emotional, and nurturing.

THE WAKAN-TANKA

At the heart of the Wheel lies an S-shape within a circle, the symbol of the life-giving source of everything that comes into physical existence – seemingly out of nothing. Named by the Plains Indians as Wakan-Tanka (Great Power), it can also be perceived as energy coming into form and form reverting to energy in the unending continuity of life.

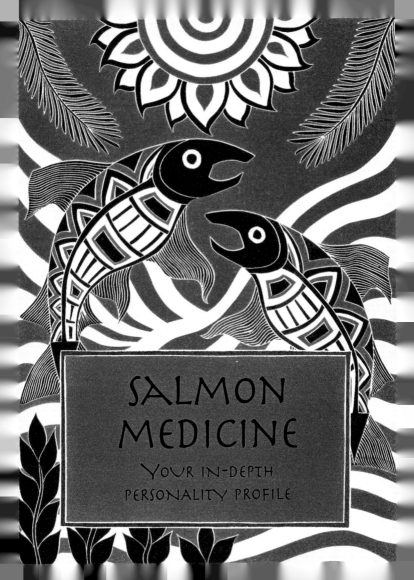

SALMON
MEDICINE

YOUR IN-DEPTH
PERSONALITY PROFILE

SEASON OF BIRTH
RIPENING TIME

THE RIPENING POWER OF SUMMER REACHES ITS PEAK
DURING THE SECOND BIRTH TIME OF THE SEASON,
LENDING THOSE BORN THEN WARMTH AND OPENNESS.

Ripening time is one of the twelve birth times, the fundamental division of the year into twelve seasonal segments (see pp.12–13). As the middle period of the Summer cycle, it is the time of year when the Sun is at its hottest and all of Nature basks in the heat of the days. Nature is bountiful and abundant during this period when the fruits of the Earth ripen.

INFLUENCE OF NATURE
The qualities and characteristics imbued in Nature at this time form the basis of your own nature. So, just as Nature is opening up in response to the continuing warmth of the season, if you were born during Ripening time, you have a sunny, open nature. As Nature offers its sweet and colorful fruits, so are you outgoing, bold, and caring. You have a depth of feeling that matches the saturated colors of this time of year. In fact, the strength of your feelings makes you more vulnerable to emotional upsets than most people, and endows you with a fiery temper, which is triggered when someone you love or something you have gained is threatened.

During this period, the Iroquois people celebrated the first crop of fresh green corn. Known as the Busk ceremony, it offered thanks for the harvest and included dancing around a sacred fire and a celebratory feast.

This show of appreciation of Nature's bounty is reflected in your own need to be appreciated. You thrive on the love and affection afforded you by others and the sense that you are needed by them.

STAGE OF LIFE
This time of year might be compared to the time of life when adulthood is becoming established. In human development terms it is a period when confidence is high and the desire to go out into the world and make your mark is great. Inevitably, disappointments accompany such a bold approach to life. Such setbacks help the young adult to mature.

ACHIEVE YOUR POTENTIAL
Your bold, enthusiastic, and warm nature makes you a natural leader. You are happy to accept the mantle of responsibility and enjoy managing

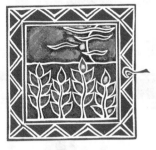

Nature's energy
The ripening aspect of Nature comes to the fore in this, the middle cycle of Summer. In the long, warm Summer days, the sweet fruits ripen, ready for picking, and the corn matures, ready for harvesting.

projects or people and the respect and admiration that brings. Beware, however, that your confidence and pride do not cause you to be so wedded to your own ideas that you cannot be objective about them or appreciate the ideas or feelings of others. Do not allow the flattery of others to blind you to their true nature or the real value of their work, and try not to let the failure of a project or relationship make you gloomy for too long.

"Life is a circle from childhood to childhood; so it is with everything where power moves." Black Elk teaching

BIRTH TOTEM
THE SALMON

THE ESSENTIAL NATURE AND CHARACTERISTIC BEHAVIOR OF THE SALMON EXPRESSES THE PERSONALITY TYPE OF THOSE BORN DURING RIPENING TIME.

Like the salmon, people born during Ripening time are confident, enthusiastic, and determined. If you were born at this time, you are likely to have a warm, courageous, optimistic nature that thrives on zestful activity and vibrant relationships.

Your love of challenges, along with your self-confidence, leads you to embark on difficult tasks with enthusiasm. This means that you often find yourself swimming against the tide. Firm in your convictions and forthright in your opinions, you are a forceful and natural leader. Thus you have little problem convincing others that yours is the correct view and your lead the one to follow.

You are flamboyant and love to dramatize situations. This can sometimes lead to impulsive behavior or poorly judged decisions. Try to develop a more cautious attitude and reflect more on the consequences of your actions.

Salmon power
Powerful and determined, the salmon also expresses the independent, courageous, and fast-moving aspects of the self-confident, flamboyant, and emotional people born at this time.

Generous and loving, you invest enormous emotional energy in your relationships and make a loyal friend and colleague. However, your belief in others' good nature as well as your own desire for love and attention make you easy to deceive. Try to cultivate a more cautious attitude toward others.

HEALTH MATTERS

You take pride in your appearance and consider the maintenance of good health and physical fitness important. Consequently, you are rarely ill and have good recuperative powers. However, your tendency to drive yourself too hard can make you prone to accidents and to suffer from stress disorders, such as high blood pressure.

THE SALMON AND
RELATIONSHIPS

VIBRANT AND ENTHUSIASTIC, SALMON PEOPLE ARE OFTEN
VERY POPULAR. THEY MAKE GENEROUS AND LOVING
PARTNERS BUT MAY BE DOMINEERING.

Forceful and flamboyant, Salmon people, like their totem animal, are not easily daunted. They are natural leaders and can be very charismatic, drawing others around them with ease. If your birth totem is Salmon, you are a warm and exciting friend. However, your determined attitude and belief that you always know best may seem arrogant. Tuning in to others' emotional needs, rather than trying to run their lives, will help you forge more balanced relationships.

LOVING RELATIONSHIPS
Although Salmon people seem very confident and self-reliant, they often rely on outside approval to feel any sense of self-worth. Emotionally vulnerable, they need love and attention in order to thrive. Male

Salmon is optimistic but tends to be egotistical, while female Salmon can be captivating but vain. Both can be demonstrative and passionate lovers.

When problems arise, it is often due to your tendency to dominate and your conviction that you are right. You will create a healthier partnership if you learn to be more flexible and tolerant.

COPING WITH SALMON
Salmon people are outwardly arrogant at times but often suffer from low self-esteem. Offer them genuine praise, not empty flattery, to earn their trust. They are impatient, so get to the point quickly and listen to their opinions attentively. When challenging their views, show them respect and consideration – they are more fragile than they seem.

SALMON IN LOVE

Salmon with Falcon This volatile couple will find romance and excitement but there may be hurt pride from time to time.

Salmon with Beaver Both try to dominate, but they have a warm affinity. Beaver's constancy can help Salmon to become more focused.

Salmon with Deer This can be a lively if rather reckless relationship with both aiming to live life to the full.

Salmon with Woodpecker Passionate Salmon should warm to Woodpecker's pampering and understand Woodpecker's deepest needs.

Salmon with Salmon This may start out as a seductive and sensual relationship, but Salmon can be overpowering, and it may become a tense partnership.

Salmon with Brown Bear Salmon's demanding nature may be too much for Brown Bear's adaptability, so Salmon may grow resentful and feel inadequate.

Salmon with Crow Both yearn for love and can be supportive. Together, they can make an exciting match.

Salmon with Snake Salmon may find Snake too intense and Snake dislikes Salmon's arrogance. Both tend to make a drama out of a crisis.

Salmon with Owl Each has the passion and persistence to satisfy each other's needs and to find new and exciting experiences in life.

Salmon with Goose Salmon's fervor arouses Goose's respect. If Goose can satisfy Salmon's ego, they can get along well.

Salmon with Otter Otter's independence can make Salmon feel belittled, but they can be a dynamic team.

Salmon with Wolf Salmon's charm can make Wolf feel special, but Salmon may be too dominant for Wolf.

DIRECTIONAL TOTEM
THE MOUSE

THE MOUSE SYMBOLIZES THE INFLUENCE OF THE SOUTH ON SALMON PEOPLE, WHOSE ENERGETIC BEHAVIOR IS DRIVEN BY THEIR STRONGLY FELT EMOTIONS.

Long Days time, Ripening time, and Harvesting time all fall within the quarter of the Medicine Wheel associated with the South Direction or Wind. The South is aligned with Summer and the bright warmth of midday, and it is associated with trust and innocence, depth of feeling, a sense of wonder, and hope. The power of the South's influence is primarily with the emotions, and its principal function is the power of giving. It takes as its totem the sensitive, curious, easily overlooked mouse.

The specific influence of the South on Salmon people is on trusting your feelings and intuition during times of change, especially

Warrior mouse doll
This Hopi Kachina doll represents the mouse, which is associated with emotional sensitivity.

when experiencing problems as you strive to mature in wisdom and self-knowledge. With the Sun at its most powerful, the South is thought to endow those born at this time with energy, creativity, and a sunny personality.

MOUSE CHARACTERISTICS

The mouse has whiskers that make it particularly sensitive to its surroundings via touch, so Native Americans believed it symbolized the power of perception through closeness to things and through feelings. Its tiny size means it may be disregarded – just as we often overlook the small, true voice of our inner self. It also expresses curiosity, the value of experiencing through exploration and involvement, and a capacity to learn and develop at considerable speed.

The spirit of the South

The Sun is at its zenith in the South, symbolizing joy in life; the Mouse totem signifies heightened perception.

If your Directional totem is Mouse, you are likely to be highly sensitive to atmosphere. Your actions are often influenced by your emotions, which you need to balance with reason. You have a good eye for detail and the ability to learn rapidly, and know that great things may grow from small beginnings. Your energy means you often take the lead, tackling difficult tasks that others avoid and accepting responsibility.

ELEMENTAL TOTEM
THE HAWK

LIKE THE HAWK, WHICH SEIZES ITS PREY AT SPEED,
SALMON PEOPLE'S SELF-CONFIDENT AND FORCEFUL
NATURE MEANS THEY ENJOY A CHALLENGE.

The Elemental Aspect of Salmon people is Fire. They share this Aspect with Falcon and Owl people, who all therefore belong to the same Elemental family or "clan" (see pp.20–21 for an introduction to the influence of the Elements). Each Elemental clan has a totem to provide insight into its essential qualities and characteristics.

THE HAWK CLAN

The totem of the Elemental clan of Fire is Hawk, which symbolizes an impulsive and enthusiastic nature with a pioneering spirit.

The hawk is quick and clear-sighted, swooping on its prey suddenly, seizing every opportunity. So, if you belong to this clan, you will have a lively personality, are happy to take the lead, and have

Spark of vitality
The hawk symbolizes the key qualities of Fire: energy and enthusiasm.

quick and very intuitive powers of understanding.

Optimistic, impulsive, and creative, you are excited by fresh ventures and fire others with the inspirational force of your enthusiasm. You dislike feeling restricted, bored, or bogged down by routine. You are often motivated by sudden flashes of inspiration, so you crave stimulation and new challenges to capture your imagination.

ELEMENTAL PROFILE

For Salmon people, the predominant Elemental Aspect of enthusiastic Fire is fundamentally affected by the qualities of your Principal Element – sensitive Water. So, if you were born at this time, you are likely to have a self-confident, outgoing, sunny personality, coupled with sensitivity and the ability to feel deep emotion.

You may have a tendency to seem arrogant and overconfident on occasion, driven by the ardor of Fire

Fire of Water
The Element of Fire feeds Water, generating enthusiasm and emotional sensitivity.

and the surging power of Water. So you may sometimes become involved in confrontations or unintentionally aggravate those closest to you, leaving you feeling misunderstood and emotionally upset. At times like these, or when you are feeling low or over-stressed, try the following revitalizing exercise. Your affinity with Fire means you respond to the warming energy of the Sun, or to the air that has been cleansed by a storm. Find a quiet, open spot outside, away from traffic, pollution, and other people. In Winter, sit by an open fire and look into the heart of the flames.

Breathe slowly and deeply, letting the brightness of the Sun or the fire warm you. With each in-breath, feel the energizing power of the life force bringing you inner light, recharging your body, mind, and spirit.

STONE AFFINITY
CARNELIAN

BY USING THE GEMSTONE WITH WHICH YOUR OWN
ESSENCE RESONATES, YOU CAN TAP INTO THE POWER OF
THE EARTH ITSELF AND AWAKEN YOUR INNER STRENGTHS.

Gemstones are precious minerals that are formed deep within the Earth itself in an exceedingly slow but continuous process. Native Americans valued gemstones not only for their natural beauty but also for being literally part of the Earth, and therefore possessing part of its life force. They regarded gemstones as being "alive" – channelers of energy that could be used in many different ways: to heal, to protect, or for meditation.

Every gemstone has a different energy or vibration. On the Medicine Wheel, a stone is associated with each birth time, the energy of which

Polished carnelian

*Carnelian, also called
cornelian, is thought to calm
the temper and strengthen
family unity.*

resonates with the essence of those born during that time. Because of this energy affiliation, your gemstone can be used to help bring you into greater harmony with the Earth and to create balance within yourself. It can also enhance and develop your good qualities and endow you with the qualities or abilities you need.

ENERGY RESONANCE
Salmon people have an affinity with carnelian – a translucent, reddish orange form of chalcedony. Carnelian has a vibrant quality that stimulates curiosity and enhances the mind's analytical powers, and it

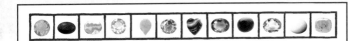

ACTIVATE YOUR GEMSTONE

Obtain a piece of carnelian and cleanse it by holding it under cold running water. Allow it to dry naturally. Then, holding the stone with both hands, bring it up to your mouth and blow into it sharply and hard, three or four times in order to impregnate it with your breath. Next, hold it firmly in one hand, and silently welcome it into your life as a friend and helper.

When you are faced with a problem, use the carnelian to help you meditate on the issue. Find a quiet spot to sit without fear of interruption and take the carnelian in your left hand, which receives subtle energies. Focus on the problem, and with the help of your affinity stone, seek a solution. Listen for the still, small voice of your inner self.

also stimulates action. It is associated with integrity by some Native Americans, who use it to dispel apathy and to free people from sorrow and envy. It is also valued for its general curative powers.

Carnelian power

To benefit most from its effect, carry or wear a piece of carnelian. It is believed to promote contentment, so keep it with you at all times.

If your birth totem is Salmon, you will find carnelian especially useful in softening anger and dispersing troubled emotions. It also helps develop self-control, making it a valuable aid in situations where you may act impulsively or without thinking, or when you find yourself being domineering.

> *"The outline of the stone is round; the power of the stone is endless."* Lakota Sioux teaching

TREE AFFINITY
YEW

GAIN A DEEPER UNDERSTANDING OF YOUR OWN NATURE
AND AWAKEN POWERS LYING DORMANT WITHIN YOU BY
RESPECTING AND CONNECTING WITH YOUR AFFINITY TREE.

Trees have an important part to play in the protection of Nature's mechanisms and in the maintenance of the Earth's atmospheric balance, which is essential for the survival of the human race.

Native Americans referred to trees as "Standing People" because they stand firm, obtaining strength from their connection with the Earth. They therefore teach us the importance of being grounded, while at the same time listening to and reaching for our higher aspirations. When respected as living beings, trees can provide insight into the workings of Nature and our own inner selves.

On the Medicine Wheel, each birth time is associated with a particular kind of tree, the basic qualities of which complement the nature of those born during that time. Salmon people have an affinity with the yew. Sometimes living for 1,000 years or more, the yew is sacred in many cultures and signifies continuity in the face of change. It tolerates unpromising conditions,

CONNECT WITH YOUR TREE

Appreciate the beauty of your affinity tree and study its nature carefully, for it has an affinity with your own nature.

The yew is a dense, slow-growing evergreen with dark green, needle-like leaves and poisonous black seeds. Yew wood is very strong and durable, and resists water; it was once valued for its use in making archers' bows and ship masts.

Try the following exercise when you need to revitalize your inner strength. Stand beside your affinity tree. Place the palms of your hands on its trunk and rest your forehead on the backs of your hands. Inhale slowly and let energy from the tree's roots flow through your body. If easily available, obtain a cutting or twig from your affinity tree to keep as a totem or helper.

and can be an inspiration to Salmon people when faced with setbacks to their ambitious plans. Salmon people sometimes find it hard to maintain continuity in their lives, but they can tap into their own powers of consistency by connecting with their tree (see panel above).

LEARNING FROM THE PAST

If your birth totem is Salmon, you are bold and confident, and have natural leadership qualities. At times,

your determination may make you seem uncompromising, arrogant, or egotistic. Your focus on the final goal means you may lose sight of the valuable experiences that have brought you so far on your journey.

Draw on the yew's powers of continuity and calm strength to help you look deep within yourself and rediscover valuable lessons from your past. Incorporate the knowledge you gain from them into your approach to achieving your goals.

"All healing plants are given by Wakan-Tanka; therefore they are holy." Lakota Sioux teaching

COLOR AFFINITY
RED

ENHANCE YOUR POSITIVE QUALITIES BY USING THE
POWER OF YOUR AFFINITY COLOR TO AFFECT YOUR
EMOTIONAL AND MENTAL STATES.

ach birth time has an affinity with a particular color. This is the color that resonates best with the energies of the people born during that time. Exposure to your affinity color will encourage a positive emotional and mental response, while exposure to colors that clash with your affinity color will have a negative effect on your entire sense of well-being.

Red resonates with Salmon people. A powerful, energetic force, red is associated with courage, vitality, and passion. It is the embodiment of self-confidence and assertiveness, of stamina and determination to continue the pursuit of goals

Color scheme
Experience the full benefit of your color affinity. Let a red color theme be the thread that runs through your whole home, from the furniture and ornaments to the walls and floors.

REFLECT ON YOUR COLOR

Take a red floating candle and place in a small bowl of water. Sit in a room where you will not be disturbed for half an hour, and place the bowl containing the candle on a table or flat surface directly in front of you.

Light the candle to release its color energy into the atmosphere. Relax in the tranquillity of the room as you focus on your affinity color and the flickering flame. Breathe slowly and rhythmically, and feel your affinity color being absorbed into your body. Allow any thoughts and sensations to flow through your mind and body: experience and reflect on them as they occur.

and ambitions despite opposition or setbacks. Red arouses the strength and passion to live life to the full – to have the courage of your convictions and the confidence to view life as an adventure and accept the challenges it sets you.

COLOR BENEFITS

Strengthen your aura and enhance your positive qualities by introducing shades of red – cherry, crimson, magenta – to the interior decor of your home. Spots of color can make all the difference. A red-tinted lampshade, for example, can alter the ambience of a room, or try placing red-patterned cushions on the chairs and sofas.

If you need a confidence boost, wear something that contains red. Whenever your energies are low, practice the color reflection exercise outlined above to balance your emotions, awaken your creativity, and help you to feel joyful.

"The power of the spirit should be honored with its color." Lakota Sioux teaching

WORKING THE WHEEL
LIFE PATH

CONSIDER YOUR BIRTH PROFILE AS A STARTING POINT IN
THE DEVELOPMENT OF YOUR CHARACTER AND THE
ACHIEVEMENT OF PERSONAL FULFILLMENT.

E ach of the twelve birth
times is associated with a
particular path of learning or
with a collection of lessons to be
learned through life. By following
your path of learning, you will
develop strengths in place of
weaknesses, achieve a greater sense
of harmony with the world, and
discover inner peace.

YOUR PATH OF LEARNING
For Salmon people, the first
lesson on your path of
learning is to cultivate a

more adaptable approach to life.
Without losing your keenly felt sense
of purpose, learn to be more flexible
in the way you attain your goals.
There is always more than one way
to reach your destination, and
whatever path you travel, you will
always have to negotiate obstacles
on the way. Cultivate patience and
tolerance so that you are less at the
mercy of your strongly
felt emotions and

*"Each man's road is
shown to him within his
own heart. There he sees all
the truths of life."* Cheyenne teaching

more easily able to find ways around problems and to make sound judgements about situations and people.

Salmon people must also learn to build up their self-esteem. The certainty and forcefulness of your personality make you appear supremely self-confident. In fact, you depend enormously on the praise and admiration of others to maintain your sense of self-worth. This makes you over-dependent on others' opinion of you and susceptible to flattery and deceit. Learn to trust in your ability to act with integrity.

Your third lesson is to achieve greater emotional harmony in your relationships by giving and receiving love in equal part. You often find yourself in emotionally traumatic waters. These are often the result of your own scant regard for the emotional needs of others. Try to avoid running other people's lives for them, and listen to their desires.

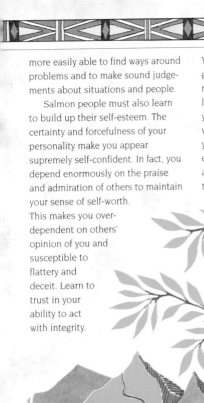

WORKING THE WHEEL
MEDICINE POWER

HARNESS THE POWERS OF OTHER BIRTH TIMES TO
TRANSFORM YOUR WEAKNESSES INTO STRENGTHS AND
TO MEET THE CHALLENGES IN YOUR LIFE.

The whole spectrum of human qualities and abilities is represented on the Medicine Wheel. The totems and affinities associated with each birth time indicate the basic qualities with which those born at that time are equipped.

Complementary affinity
A key strength of Otter – weak in Salmon – is the ability to be idealistic and altruistic.

Study your path of learning (see pp.42–43) to identify aspects of your personality that may need to be strengthened, then look at other birth times to discover the totems and affinities that can assist you in this task. For example, your personal Elemental profile is Fire of Water (see pp.34–35), so for balance you need the freedom of movement of Air and the stabilizing, persistent qualities of Earth. Crow's Elemental profile is Air of Earth and Goose's is Earth of Air, so meditate on these birth totems. In addition, you may find it useful to study the profiles of the other two members of your Elemental clan of Hawk – Falcon and Owl – to discover how the same Elemental Aspect of Fire can be expressed differently.

Also helpful is the birth totem opposite yours on the Wheel, which contains qualities that complement or enhance your own. This is known as your complementary affinity, which for Salmon people is Otter.

ESSENTIAL STRENGTHS

D escribed below are the essential strengths of each birth totem. To develop a quality that is weak in yourself or that you need to meet a particular challenge, meditate upon the birth totem that contains the attribute you need. Obtain a representation of the relevant totem – a claw, tooth, or feather; a picture, ring, or model. Affirm that the power it represents is within you.

Falcon medicine is the power of keen observation and the ability to act decisively and energetically whenever action is required.

Beaver medicine is the ability to think creatively and laterally – to develop alternative ways of doing or thinking about things.

Deer medicine is characterized by sensitivity to the intentions of others and to that which might be detrimental to your well-being.

Woodpecker medicine is the ability to establish a steady rhythm throughout life and to be tenacious in protecting all that you value.

Salmon medicine is the strength to be determined and courageous in the choice of goals you want to achieve and to have enough stamina to see a task through to the end.

Brown Bear medicine is the ability to be resourceful, hardworking, and dependable in times of need, and to draw on inner strength.

Crow medicine is the ability to transform negative or nonproductive situations into positive ones and to transcend limitations.

Snake medicine is the talent to adapt easily to changes in circumstances and to manage transitional phases well.

Owl medicine is the power to see clearly during times of uncertainty and to conduct life consistently, according to long-term plans.

Goose medicine is the courage to do whatever might be necessary to protect your ideals and to adhere to your principles in life.

Otter medicine is the ability to connect with your inner child, to be innovative and idealistic, and to thoroughly enjoy the ordinary tasks and routines of everyday life.

Wolf medicine is the courage to act according to your intuition and instincts rather than your intellect, and to be compassionate.